PEYOTE ST[

A comprehen

pictures to lea   ...cric peyote
beading stitch techniques and patterns
and produce stunning stitch beading
projects

Mitchell Caleb

Table of contents

CHAPTER ONE

    Introduction to peyote stitch beading

    Definition of Peyote Stitch Beading

    History of Peyote Stitch Beading

    Benefits of Beading with Peyote Stitch

CHAPTER TWO

    Tools and materials needed

    How to Get Started with Beading Using the Peyote Stitch

CHAPTER THREE

    Basic Peyote Stitch Techniques

    How to work Even Count Peyote Stitch

    Peyote Stitch with Odd Counts

    Working Flat peyote stitch

    Working tubular Peyote stitch

CHAPTER FOUR

    Guide to creating Flat Even Count Peyote Stitch

CHAPTER FIVE

    GUIDE TO MAKING PEYOTE STITCH BEAD BRACELET

CHAPTER ONE

Introduction to peyote stitch beading

Beadwork with the peyote stitch is a common method that's used to make gorgeous jewelry and other items out of beadwork. Beadwork fans of all levels, from novices to seasoned professionals, have shown interest in purchasing it due to the complex patterns and motifs it has. Peyote stitch has a long and illustrious history that spans back centuries and has its origins in the culture of Native Americans. It has grown in popularity in recent years as a means of releasing one's creative side and de-stressing from the pressures and demands of modern life. This detailed tutorial will walk you through the basics of peyote stitch beadwork, from its history to the equipment and supplies you'll need, as well as the step-by-step directions you need to perfect this stunning technique. This tutorial will give you with all you need to know to make magnificent pieces of jewelry and accessories, regardless of how much expertise you have in beading. So, let's go right into the exciting world of beading with the peyote stitch, shall we?

Definition of Peyote Stitch Beading

Beadwork using the peyote stitch is a common method that includes stitching beads together in a precise pattern using a needle and thread. This technique is known as the peyote stitch beading. The stitch produces a woven appearance, which may be used in the production of a wide range of jewelry and accessories, including necklaces, bracelets, earrings, and many more. Peyote stitch is a flexible pattern that can be used to make a variety of forms and designs. It is defined by its stacked rows of beads that produce a consistent, flat surface. Peyote stitch may be used to create diverse shapes and motifs. It is a flexible stitch that can be done in several versions such as even count peyote stitch and odd count peyote stitch, and it can be used with a range of bead sizes and kinds to create elaborate patterns and designs. For example, even count peyote stitch can be done with even bead counts, while odd count peyote stitch may be done with odd bead counts.

History of Peyote Stitch Beading

Beadwork using the peyote stitch has a rich history that extends back centuries and has its origins in the culture of Native Americans. The Huichol people of Mexico employed the stitch, as did other Native American tribes from the Great Plains area of North America, such as the Lakota, Cheyenne, and Comanche. In addition, the stitch was used in Guatemala.

The complex beading for ceremonial reasons, such as prayer fans, medicine bags, and headdresses, was originally created using the peyote stitch by Native American beaders. In Native American culture, the usage of peyote stitch was often connected to religious and spiritual rituals and was seen as a kind of prayer and meditation.

The peyote cactus, which was revered in many Native American civilizations and was often included into spiritual rituals, inspired the naming of this particular stitch. The peyote cactus may be found in the southwestern United States. It was thought that the use of the peyote stitch in beading was a method to connect with the spiritual realm and was a representation of the connectivity of all things in the universe.

Peyote stitch has developed through time to include a broad variety of different motifs and styles, becoming more popular in beading outside of the context of Native American culture as it spread. Peyote stitch is a well-known beading method that is used by professionals and amateurs from all over the globe to make exquisitely detailed works of jewelry and other accessories.

Benefits of Beading with Peyote Stitch

Beadwork using the peyote stitch provides its practitioners with a number of advantages, including the following:

1. Beadwork with the peyote stitch is an excellent method to de-stress and unwind at the end of a long and stressful day. Stitching beads may be a soothing and contemplative activity that can help relieve feelings of tension and anxiety.

2. Expression of Creativity: Peyote stitch beadwork gives you the opportunity to showcase your creative side and produce one-of-a-kind items

of jewelry and other accessories. You may create your own unique designs and patterns by playing with with the various colors, shapes, and dimensions of the beads.

3. Beadwork with the peyote stitch takes focus and attention to detail, both of which may help you develop a more attentive attitude and increase your ability to concentrate.

4. Pride in One's Work and a Sense of achievement: When you finish a beading project using the peyote stitch, you may feel a sense of achievement and take pride in one's work. It has the potential to be an excellent method for enhancing one's self-esteem and confidence.

5. Beading using the peyote stitch can be a social pastime, enabling you to interact with other beaders and share your enthusiasm for the art with them. You may meet other people who share your interests by participating in beading groups, going to seminars and events, or both.

Beadwork with the peyote stitch has various advantages to your physical health, mental health, and social life, all of which may contribute to an overall improvement in your quality of life and well-being.

CHAPTER TWO

Tools and materials needed

Beadwork with the peyote stitch requires a few essential equipment and supplies to get started, including the following:

Tools:

1. A thin, long needle with a tiny eye that is designed to fit through the holes in the beads is referred to as a beading needle.

2. Beading Thread is a robust and long-lasting thread that does not fray or break apart easily. Nymo and Fireline are two choices that are often used.

3. To cut the thread, you will need a pair of scissors that are very sharp.

4. A bead mat is a cushioned surface that is designed to stop beads from rolling away and to improve visibility of the beads themselves.

Materials:

1. Beads: Select beads in the size, shape, and color of your choosing. Due to the consistency of their sizes and shapes, Miyuki Delica beads are a popular choice for the peyote stitch.

2. A clasp is a kind of closing that you may use on your final product. Some examples of clasps are a lobster clasp or a toggle clasp.

3. Jump Rings are a kind of little metal ring that are used in the process of attaching the clasp to the completed item.

4. Optional: Using a thread conditioner, such as Thread Heaven or beeswax, will assist avoid tangling and keep the thread from fraying. Both of these problems are common when working with thread.

Beading with the peyote stitch just requires a few simple tools and supplies, so you should have all you need to get started right away. As you get more skill, you will be able to construct more intricate designs and patterns by experimenting with a wider variety of beads, threads, and tools to make your creations.

How to Get Started with Beading Using the Peyote Stitch

If you've never done beadwork using the peyote stitch before, the following instructions should help you get started:

1. Select a Pattern: To begin, select a pattern that you'd want to create for your project. You may search for patterns on the internet or in books, or you can design your own.

2. Beads, thread, needles, and a beading mat are some of the things you'll need to get started on your project. Make sure you have all of these things on hand before you begin.

3. Cut your thread: To begin, you will need to cut a piece of thread that is an appropriate working length for you,

which is normally between 4-6 feet in length. Prepare your needle by threading it, and then tie a knot at the very end of the thread.

4. Begin your first row: To begin your first row, pick up a certain amount of beads in accordance with the instructions provided for the design. You should have a tail of a few inches once you have finished sliding the beads down to the knot at the end of your thread. To make a loop, you will need to put your needle through the beads again, but this time in the other direction.

5. Continue stitching: To construct the second row, pick up the amount of beads given in the design, and then run your needle through the final bead in

the row that was created before. Proceed to stitch rows in this manner until the required length has been achieved.

6. Putting the finishing touches on your item To put the finishing touches on your piece, add a clasp and jump rings to either end. Make sure your knot is firm, and then cut off any extra thread.

Beadwork with the peyote stitch gives you the opportunity to create complex patterns that are one-of-a-kind if you are willing to experiment with the many different versions of the stitch as well as the many different kinds of beads.

CHAPTER THREE

Basic Peyote Stitch Techniques

Beadwork with the peyote stitch may be accomplished using the following fundamental techniques:

1. Even count Peyote stitch- this involves working with an even number of stitches per row, this particular form of the peyote stitch is by far the most prevalent. Create a foundation row by stringing together an even number of beads to begin. At the beginning of each next row, take up a bead and thread it through the space between the two beads in the row below. You will need to continue sewing in this manner, changing the orientation of the rows, until you achieve the length that you wish.

2. Peyote stitch with an odd number of beads per row The odd-count peyote stitch is quite similar to the even-count peyote stitch, with the exception that it begins with an odd number of beads in the foundation row. To get started, make a foundation row that has an even number of beads and an odd number of beads. For the subsequent rows, add a bead and pass through the next two beads in the previous row, alternating the direction of the rows.

3. The flat peyote stitch is used to produce flat objects, such as bracelets and necklaces. This stitch is also known as the flat peyote weave. To begin, string a row of beads at the bottom of the foundation. In the rows that follow, you will need to add another bead and then go on to the next bead in the row

below. To make a flat item, alternate the direction in which the rows are worked.

4. The peyote stitch known as the tubular peyote stitch is used to make cylindrical objects like necklaces and bracelets. To get started, make a foundation row of beads by stringing them around in a circle. In the rows that follow, you will need to add another bead and then go on to the next bead in the row below. Carry on stitching in this manner while increasing the row count until the item reaches the desired length.

5. Reducing: When adding a new bead, skip one or more of the beads in the row below it. This will allow you to

bring the total number of beads in a row down.

6. Increasing: When beginning a new row of beads, you should add more than one bead at a time in order to achieve the desired result of increasing the number of beads in each row.

These fundamental skills serve as the cornerstone for a wide variety of peyote stitch beading patterns. When you have more experience, you'll be able to create designs and patterns that are more intricate using these methods.

How to work Even Count Peyote Stitch

The even count peyote stitch is a well-known variation of the peyote stitch that results in a piece that is both flat and flexible. This is the procedure to follow:

Materials needed:

• Beads of your choosing (optional)

• A thread for beading

• Beading needle

• Scissors

• Bead mat

Instructions:

1. Start with an even number of beads: To begin the even count peyote stitch, you need to start with an even number of beads. The quantity of beads you need depends depend on the size of your creation.

2. Create the first row: Pick up the first two beads and slide them down to the end of your thread. Pass your needle through the second bead in the other way to make a loop. This will be the first two beads of your first row.

3. Create the second row: Pick up one bead and feed your needle through the second bead in the previous row. Pick up another bead and run your needle through the next bead in the preceding row. Continue sewing in this fashion until you reach the end of the row.

4. produce following rows: To produce future rows, you'll need to alternate between sewing through the first and second beads in the preceding row. Pick up one bead and feed your needle through the next bead in the preceding

row. Pick up another bead and feed your needle through the next bead in the preceding row, alternating between the first and second beads.

5. End your work: When you've completed your piece, weave your thread through a few beads to fasten it. Tie a knot and snip off any extra thread.

With patience, you can make elaborate patterns with even count peyote stitch. Experiment with various bead colors and designs to make unique pieces of jewelry.

Peyote Stitch with Odd Counts

Another common version of the peyote stitch, known as odd count peyote stitch, produces a fabric with a feel that is different from that produced by even count peyote stitch. This is the procedure to follow:

Materials:

- Beads of your choosing (optional)

- A thread for beading

- Beading needle

- Scissors

- Bead mat

Instructions:

1. To begin the odd count peyote stitch, you will need to begin with an odd number of beads. The quantity of beads you need depends depend on the size of your creation.

2. To make the first row, start by picking up the first three beads and

sliding them down until they are flush with the end of your thread. Pass your needle through the second bead in the other way to make a loop. These three beads will be at the beginning of your first row of beads.

3. To begin the creation of the second row, pick up one bead and thread your needle through the third bead of the row that was just completed. After picking up another bead, you should now thread your needle through the second bead that was located in the row before. Continue sewing in this fashion until you reach the end of the row.

4. produce following rows: To produce future rows, you'll need to alternate between sewing through the first and

second beads in the preceding row. Pick up one bead and feed your needle through the next bead in the preceding row. While alternating between the first and second beads, pick up another bead and feed your needle through the next bead in the row below.

5. End your work: When you've completed your piece, weave your thread through a few beads to fasten it. After completing the knot, trim away any extra thread.

Due to the fact that odd count peyote stitch includes an unequal amount of beads in each row, the finished product will have a somewhat different texture than even count peyote stitch would. Using this technique, you may make one-of-a-kind pieces of jewelry by experimenting with a wide variety of bead colors and designs.

Working Flat peyote stitch

A piece of beadwork that is flat and two-dimensional may be created using a method known as flat peyote stitch. This is the procedure to follow:

Materials:

• Beads of your choosing (optional)

• A thread for beading

• Beading needle

• Scissors

• Bead mat

Instructions:

1. To make the first row, start by picking up an even number of beads

and sliding them down until they are level with the end of your thread. To make a loop, run your needle back through the same set of beads but this time in the other direction.

2. To make the second row, begin by selecting a new bead and threading your needle through the second bead in the row below it, continuing to go in the same way as you did in the first row. Proceed with the stitching in the same manner until you reach the last space in the row.

3. Make succeeding rows: To make succeeding rows, you will need to stitch between the first and second beads of the preceding row in a randomized order. This will allow you to produce successive rows. After starting with a

fresh bead, go on to the preceding row's subsequent bead and thread your needle through it. While alternating between the first and second beads, pick up another bead and feed your needle through the next bead in the row below.

4. Finish the creation by weaving your thread through a few beads to fasten it once you have completed the component you were working on. After completing the knot, trim away any extra thread.

You may use the flat peyote stitch to make a variety of patterns and motifs, including letters and shapes. Using this technique, you may make one-of-a-kind pieces of jewelry by experimenting with a wide variety of bead colors and designs.

Working tubular Peyote stitch

The tubular peyote stitch is a method that may be used to produce beadwork in the shape of a tube or cylinder. This is the procedure to follow:

Materials:

• Beads of your choosing (optional)

• A thread for beading

• Beading needle

• Scissors

• Bead mat

Instructions:

1. To make the first row, start by picking up an even number of beads

and sliding them down until they are level with the end of your thread. To make a loop, run your needle back through the same set of beads but this time in the other direction.

2. To make the second row, begin by selecting a new bead and threading your needle through the second bead in the row below it, continuing to go in the same way as you did in the first row. After picking up another bead, move your needle so that it is heading in the opposite direction of the one it just passed through in the row below it. Proceed with the stitching in the same manner until you reach the last space in the row.

3. Make succeeding rows: To make succeeding rows, you will need to stitch

between the first and second beads of the preceding row in a randomized order. This will allow you to produce successive rows. After starting with a new bead, you will need to move your needle in the same way as previously in order to pass through the next bead on the row below. After picking up another bead, move your needle so that it is heading in the opposite direction of the one it just passed through in the row below it. Carry on sewing in this manner until the length of your piece is exactly how you want it.

4. Finish the creation by weaving your thread through a few beads to fasten it once you have completed the component you were working on. After

completing the knot, trim away any extra thread.

The tubular peyote stitch may be used to make a variety of different patterns and designs, such as ropes and straps for use in the creation of necklaces and bracelets. Using this technique, you may make one-of-a-kind pieces of jewelry by experimenting with a wide variety of bead colors and designs.

CHAPTER FOUR

Guide to creating Flat Even Count Peyote Stitch

The Flat Even Count Peyote Stitch and How to Do It

I will explain how to make flat even count peyote stitch in the next chapter and break it down step by step.

The first half of this course walks you through the process of adding a striped pattern to your beading, as well as how to beadweave in flat even count peyote stitch using seed beads. By according to these directions, you will be able to create stunning peyote stitch jewelry, such as a necklace, bracelet, ring, or earrings, for example. Peyote stitch is one of those things that, if you've never done it before, you're going to discover that you can't stop doing it!

You will need the following items in order to follow along with this tutorial:

• Toho Treasure seed beads in two distinct hues – the fact that these seed beads are very consistent in shape and size makes them ideal for the sort of beading activity that is being undertaken here. This lesson includes beads with a size 11/0 gauge, but you may substitute beads with a size 8/0 gauge if you'd like. Doing so will make this instruction simpler for those of you who are just starting out with peyote stitch.

• A beading needle in either a size 10 or a size 12.

• A beading thread like Nymo or similar.

1st Stage

Be sure you begin by putting some beading thread through the eye of your needle. When beginning your peyote stitch project, the following step is to make a stop bead. Because of this, your beading will be more secure, and you won't have to worry about seed beads falling off the end of your thread.

Pick up one seed bead with your needle, and then slip it down the thread until you have a tail of about 6 or 8 inches. This will make a stop bead for you. Repeating the previous step in the seed bead in the same direction will ensure that it is securely fastened and won't come loose. You may either weave the tail back into your beadwork or use it later to construct a clasp for the bracelet you're creating if you're in the process of making one. Be careful to use the same color bead for your initial few rows of peyote stitch that you will be using for the rest of the project.

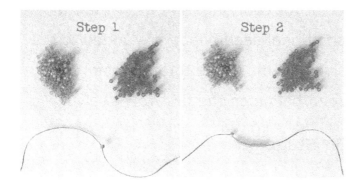

2nd Stage

After you have finished making your stop bead, proceed to choose some seed beads of the same color. The number is up to you, since it is determined by the width that is required for the project that you are working on. To use this strategy successfully, you must ensure that the number of rows you have completed, including the row that contains the stop bead, is an even number. In this guide, the stop bead serves as the starting point for counting, and after that, 11 additional seed beads are added to the string to make the total number of seed beads on the first row twelve.

3rd Stage

After you have strung on the required quantity of seed beads onto your thread, you are ready to go on to the second and third rows. When worked in peyote stitch, this will really make the third row, despite the fact that it will seem like the second row. You will need to acquire some additional beads and also make use of some of the beads that were used in the first row in order to complete the second and third rows of your pattern. When using the peyote stitch, you count the rows in a diagonal direction starting from one of the corners of your beadwork.

To begin the second and third rows, thread one seed bead of the same color onto your thread (bead 13 in this lesson). This will serve as the beginning of each row. The next step in the process involves moving backwards and skipping a bead (number 12) before returning to bead 11. Beads 12 and 13 need to be positioned such that they are sitting on top of one another, and you should make every effort to prevent them from turning the other way. Peyote stitch is significantly simpler to do once the first few rows have been completed, despite the fact that this section is rather tricky.

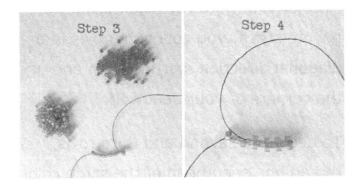

4th Stage

Carry on with the row by working backwards, picking up a new bead, skipping a bead, and proceeding through the next one as shown in the photo above. You'll soon see that your beadwork is developing a pattern that looks like a series of building blocks.

Continue to move your beadwork into position as you go so that the seed beads may sit properly on top of one another.

5th Stage

When you've finished this row, you'll really have completed rows 2 and 3, and the beading you've created should resemble somewhat like the picture to the right.

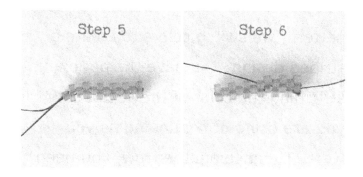

6th Stage

Proceed with the following row by skipping one seed bead, picking up a new seed bead, and proceeding through the seed bead located immediately after it. When you've finished this stage, you'll be able to count four seed beads in a row in a diagonal direction. This indicates that you'll have finished four rows in total by the time you reach this point.

7th **Stage**

In this lesson, when we have completed four rows of the same pattern, we switch colors to create a striped design. You have the option of switching the color of the seed bead you are using or continuing as you were. To make another row, you need just to repeat steps 3 through 5.

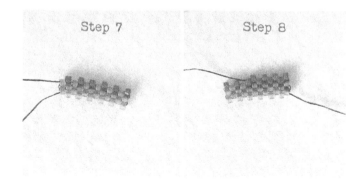

Step 7   Step 8

8th **Stage**

This beading lesson has a design that
calls for four rows of gray beads and
four rows of red beads. Continue
working three more rows until you
have a total of four rows completed;
this will give you an even stripe.

9th **Stage**

To produce more stripes for your
peyote stitch beads, just repeat steps 3
through 8.

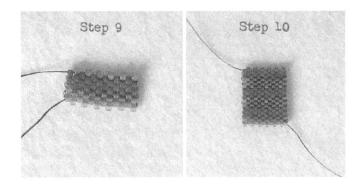

10th **Stage**

Continue working in the flat even count peyote stitch, generating stripes as you stitch until your beadwork reaches the length that you need it to be for the jewelry piece that you are working on.

I really hope that you had a good time going through this free beadweaving lesson. Please subscribe to our email so that you don't miss out on future lessons!

CHAPTER FIVE

GUIDE TO MAKING PEYOTE STITCH BEAD BRACELET

Peyote Stitch is the one that would come out on top if there was a competition to determine which bead weaving stitch had the most distinct variants. There is a huge variety of permutations that you might test.

One of the easiest Peyote Stitch beading methods is called Flat Even Count Peyote Stitch. Because you begin with an even number of beads, the beadwork that you create with this technique ends up being flat, thus the name.

In this tutorial, we are going to make a bracelet using a peyote stitch that is flat and even.

Because of their incredible uniformity in both size and shape, Delica beads come highly recommended by yours truly as a replacement for conventional seed beads in beadwork.

Materials and Supplies Required

- 14 grams of size 8/0 Miyuki Delica beads, color 1 (A)

- Ten grams of size 8/0 Miyuki Delica beads in color 2 (B).

- 18 Miyuki 11/0 seed beads in color "C"

- 1 Clasp

- Beading thread measuring 4.5 yards in length

- One beading needle in a size 10

• A flame from a thread burner or a pair of sharp scissors

• Bead mat

The whole written instruction for the beaded bracelet may be found here:

PEYOTE STITCH BRACELET INSTRUCTIONS

First Stage: thread your needle with a length of beading thread that is comfortable for you to work with.

Put on a stop bead and leave a tail that is 10 inches long.

2nd **Stage:** String together the numbers 2A, 2B, 2A, and 2A.

Allow the beads to go down the thread until they reach the stop bead.

3rd **Stage**: The third step is to string 1A.

Turn the direction of travel around and leave out the last 1A strung in Step 2.

After that, go through the subsequent 1A.

Please take note that the newly-added 1A should be stacked on top of the previous 1A.

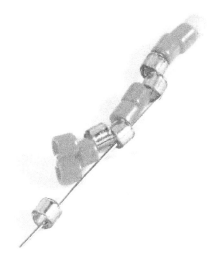

4th **Stage**: String 1B.

Proceed to the next 1B after skipping the 1B that comes after it.

5th **Stage**: The fifth step is to string 1A.

Pass through the next 1A after skipping the 1A that comes after it.

6th **Stage:** String 1B.

Proceed to the next 1B after skipping the 1B that comes after it.

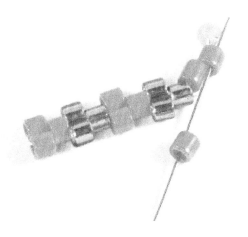

7th Stage: String the 1A.

You should skip the 1A that comes after it and go straight through the 1A that comes after it.

8th **Stage**: The eighth step is to string 1A.

Change the way you are going and, bypassing the 1A at the end of the row, go back through the preceding row's most recent addition of the 1A.

Please take note that you should be going via the 1A that is protruding.

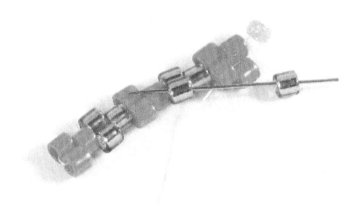

9th **Stage**: String 1B.

You should skip the 1B that comes after it and go through the 1B that is jutting out next.

Carry on until you reach the end of the row and then fill in the three empty places with the numbers 1A, 1B, and then 1A.

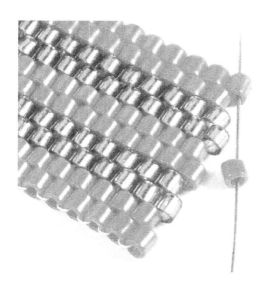

10th **Stage**: Continue to repeat Steps 8 and 9 until you have achieved the length you wish.

11th **Stage**: The clasp will be attached to the beading after you have reached the center columns of the beadwork, which is the focus of Step 11.

In the rows that come before the last two rows, you need to go through the 2A.

12th **Stage**: After that, go to the 2B squares in the rows that come before the last two rows.

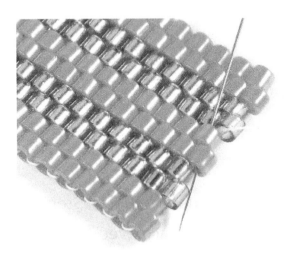

13th **Stage**: Proceed through the last 2A, which is located in the center of the beadwork.

14th **Stage:** In Step 14, you will string 5C together with one side of the clasp.

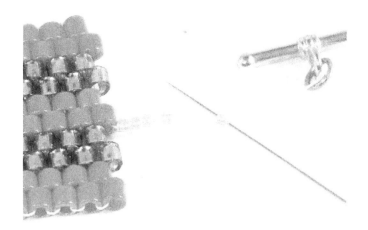

15th **Stage**: Retrace your steps via the most recent 1C string.

16th **Stage:** The 16th step is to string 4C.

From the side that is not where the thread is departing the beading, go through the 2A that is in the centre of the beadwork.

Improve the strength of the clasp.

Beadwork should be woven with the working thread in it. Make a few knots using a half-hitch technique, then cut off the excess.

17th **Stage**: Remove the stop bead from the beading that is located at the other end. Join the needle to the loose end of the thread.

To attach the other side of your clasp, you will need to repeat Steps 11-16.

Your bracelet is finished and ready to wear!

Made in the USA
Monee, IL
21 November 2023